Man meets Woman
Mann trifft Frau
Hommes/femmes, mode d'emploi
Hombre y mujer, cara a cara

A book by **Yang Liu**

Humans, so one Chinese legend tells us, were created by a female divinity. At first she made them sexless and completely identical. Only when they consequently failed to produce offspring did the goddess later furnish them with gender. According to the Bible, humans were created by a male God—first man, then woman. The world of science in turn offers us an entirely different version of the origins of humankind.

I myself have experienced, directly and indirectly, many communication problems between the two sexes, both in my private life and in my professional career. As a working wife and mother, I am compelled to realize time and time again how many minor and major differences exist between men and women, despite today's ongoing debate on the subject and the constant redefinition of male and female roles. Many of these differences arise out of traditional gender models and are dictated by social and professional structures.

With this little book I would like to present a visual documentary of my personal views on the subject of communication between men and women. I thereby hope to be able to encourage all of us to approach this subject with a little more humor and, in our daily interactions, to look at and think about things from the viewpoint of the opposite sex.

– Yang Liu

Folgt man einer chinesischen Sage, wurden die Menschen durch eine weibliche Göttin erschaffen. Zunächst waren sie geschlechtslos und absolut identisch. Erst als deshalb die Nachfahren ausblieben, hat die Göttin sie nachträglich mit dem Geschlecht ausgestattet. Der Bibel nach wurden die Menschen von Gott, einem Mann, erschaffen – zuerst der Mann, dann die Frau. Und die Wissenschaft wiederum legt uns eine ganz andere Ursprungsgeschichte der Menschheit nahe.

Ich selber habe viele Kommunikationsprobleme zwischen den beiden Geschlechtern direkt oder indirekt erlebt, sowohl im Privatleben als auch im beruflichen Alltag. Als berufstätige Ehefrau und Mutter muss ich nun immer wieder feststellen, wie viele kleine und große Unterschiede zwischen Mann und Frau existieren, trotz der fortwährenden Debatte zu dieser Thematik und der ständigen Neudefinition der Rollen. Einige dieser Unterschiede sind durch traditionelle Vorbilder geprägt sowie durch gesellschaftliche oder berufliche Strukturen bedingt.

Mit diesem Buch möchte ich eine Dokumentation meiner persönlichen Wahrnehmung zu diesem Thema präsentieren. Und ich hoffe, es regt dazu an, das Thema mit mehr Humor zu betrachten. So können wir uns im alltäglichen Umgang vielleicht dafür öffnen, Dinge einmal aus der Perspektive des anderen zu sehen und zu bedenken.

– Yang Liu

Si l'on en croit une légende chinoise, les humains ont été créés par une déesse. À l'origine, ils étaient asexués et parfaitement identiques. Comprenant qu'ils étaient alors incapables d'avoir une descendance, la divinité les dota d'un sexe distinct. Selon la Bible, les humains ont été créés par un Dieu masculin qui a d'abord façonné l'homme, puis la femme. Quant à la science, elle nous enseigne une tout autre histoire des origines de l'humanité.

Pour ma part, j'avoue avoir été souvent confrontée, plus ou moins directement, à bien des problèmes de communication entre les deux sexes, que ce soit dans ma vie privée ou professionnelle. En tant que femme active, mariée et mère de famille, je constate combien sont nombreuses les différences – petites et grandes – entre l'homme et la femme, et ce malgré l'éternel débat sur la question et en dépit d'une définition des rôles sans cesse revisitée. Bon nombre de ces différences sont le reflet de modèles traditionnels en matière de genre ou de la structure de la société et du monde du travail.

J'ai donc conçu ce petit ouvrage comme un témoignage de ma propre perception du sujet. J'espère qu'il nous incitera toutes et tous à aborder la communication hommes/femmes avec un peu d'humour et nous aidera au quotidien à considérer les choses avec le regard du sexe opposé.

– Yang Liu

Según una leyenda china, los humanos fueron creados por una diosa. Al principio no tenían sexo y todos eran exactamente iguales. Pero al no poder tener descendencia, la diosa decidió dotarlos de sexo. Según la Biblia, los seres humanos fueron creados por un Dios varón: primero hizo al hombre y luego, a la mujer. La ciencia, sin embargo, nos brinda un planteamiento completamente distinto.

Yo misma he sido testigo, directa o indirectamente, de muchos problemas de comunicación entre ambos sexos, tanto en mi vida privada como en el día a día profesional. Como esposa y madre trabajadora me doy cuenta de las pequeñas y grandes diferencias existentes entre hombres y mujeres, pese al continuo debate sobre este tema y la constante redefinición de los roles. Algunas de estas diferencias vienen marcadas tanto por los modelos tradicionales como por las estructuras sociales y profesionales.

Con este libro quiero documentar mi percepción personal sobre este tema. Espero que ayude a abordarlo con más humor y abra una ventana que permita ver y gestionar las situaciones de nuestra vida cotidiana desde el punto de vista del sexo contrario.

– Yang Liu

He thinks...
Er denkt...
Il pense...
Él piensa...

She thinks...
Sie denkt...
Elle pense...
Ella piensa...

Man to man
Von Mann zu Mann · **D'homme à homme** · *De hombre a hombre*

Woman to woman

Von Frau zu Frau · De femme à femme · *De mujer a mujer*

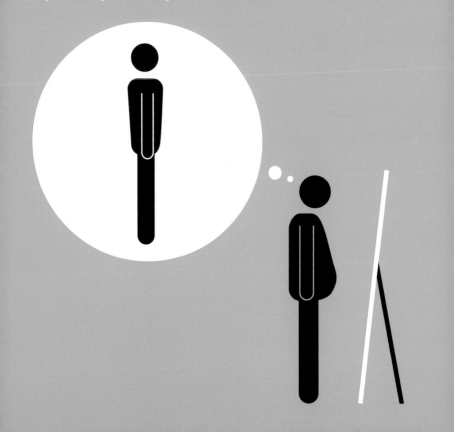

Self-image
Spiegelbild · Image de soi · *Imagen de sí misma*

Shopping
Shoppen · **Shopping** · *Compras*

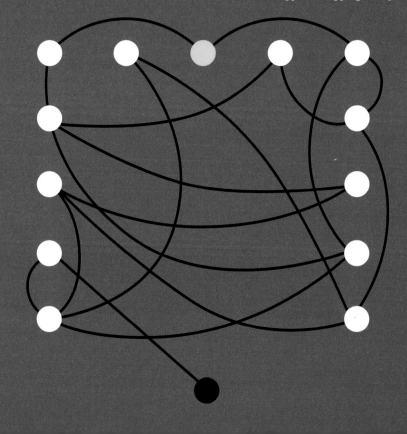

Private talk
Privatgespräch
Discussion privée
Conversaciones privadas

Private talk
Privatgespräch
Discussion privée
Conversaciones privadas

Business talk
Berufliches Gespräch
Discussion professionnelle
Conversaciones profesionales

Business talk
Berufliches Gespräch
Discussion professionnelle
Conversaciones profesionales

need
brauchen · **besoin** · *necesidad*

buy
kaufen · **achat** · *compra*

need
brauchen · besoin · *necesidad*

buy
kaufen · achat · *compra*

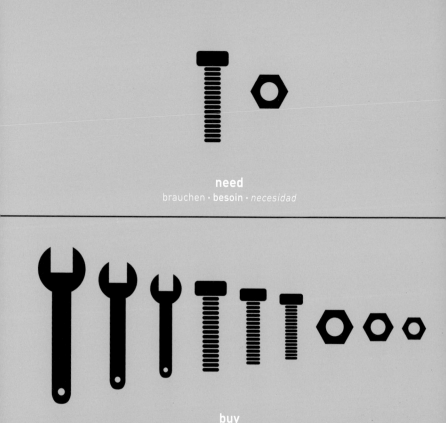

need
brauchen · **besoin** · *necesidad*

buy
kaufen · **achat** · *compra*

need
brauchen · besoin · *necesidad*

buy
kaufen · achat · *compra*

Single focus
Konzentration · Tâche unique · *Focalización*

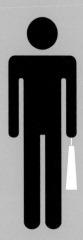

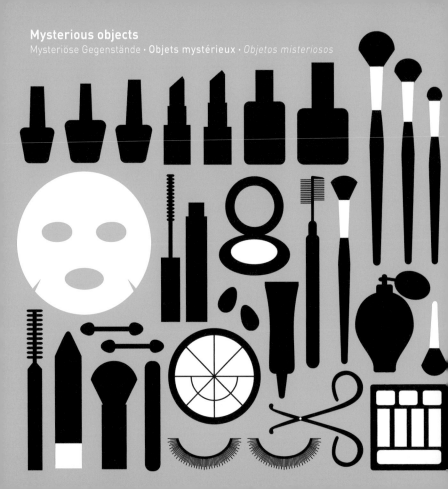

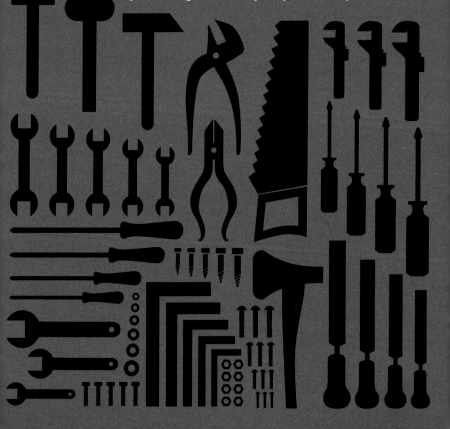

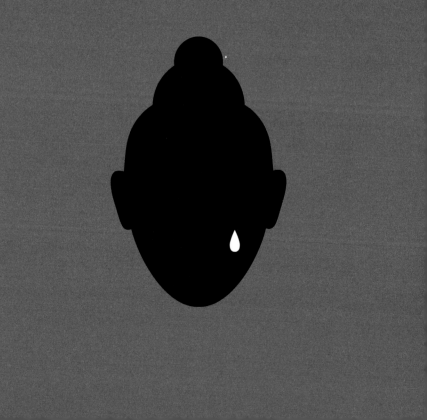

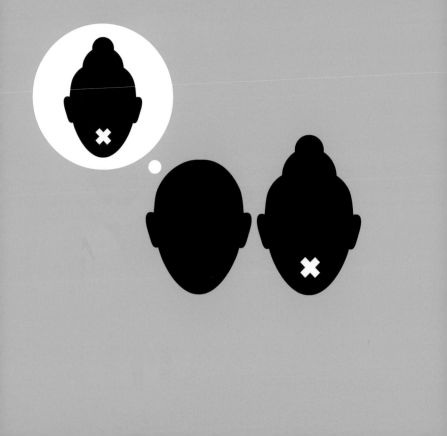

When she's silent
Wenn sie schweigt · Quand elle se tait · *Cuando ella calla*

Speaking about breaking up

Trennungsgespräch · **Parler de séparation** · *Habla de separación*

Finding the way

Er sucht den Weg · **Chercher son chemin** · *Buscando una dirección*

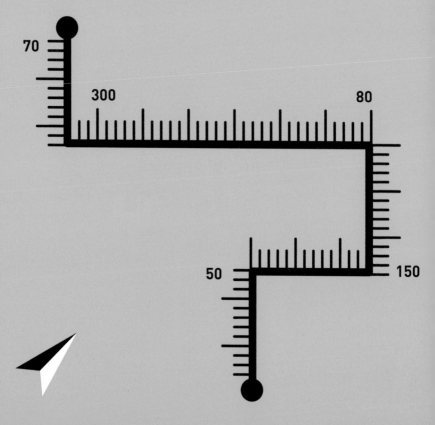

Bathroom break

Gang zur Toilette · Aller aux toilettes · *Vamos al baño*

Luggage

Gepäck · **Bagages** · *Equipaje*

Melodrama

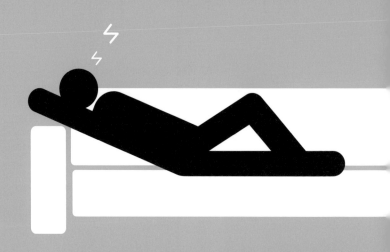

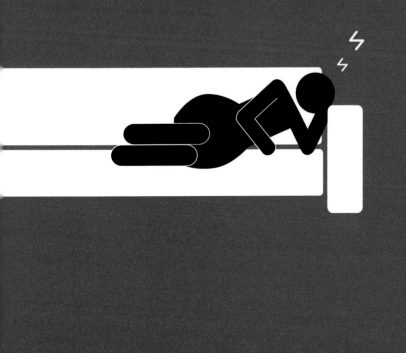

Preferences

Vorlieben · Préférences · *Prioridades*

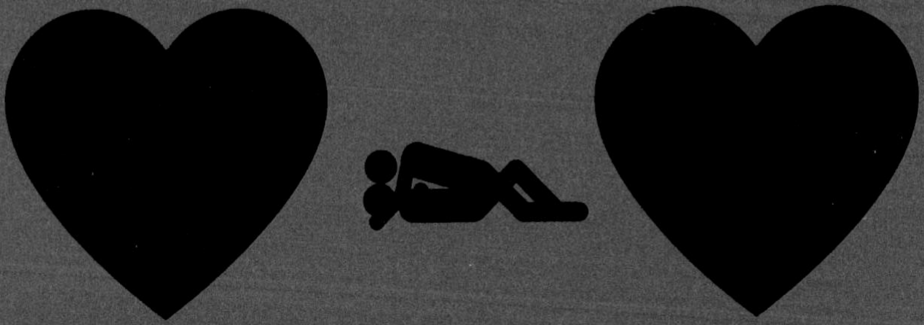

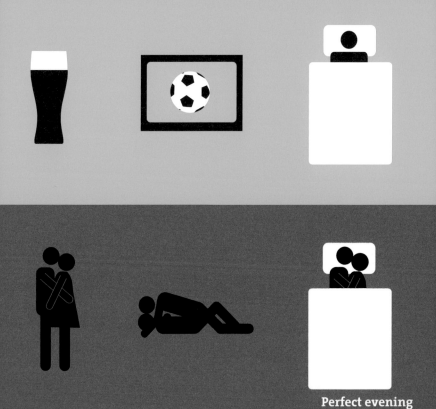

Perfect evening
Perfekter Abend · Soirée idéale · *Noche perfecta*

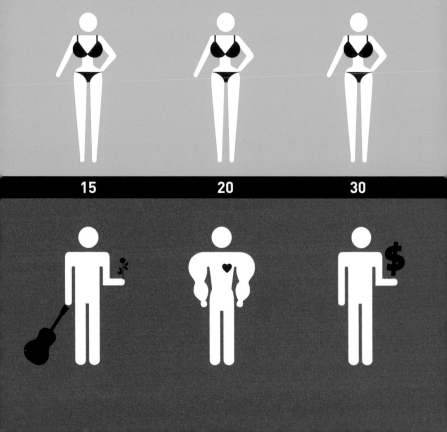

Projected dream woman
Seine Traumfrau · **Femme de ses rêves** · *La mujer de sus sueños*

15   20   30

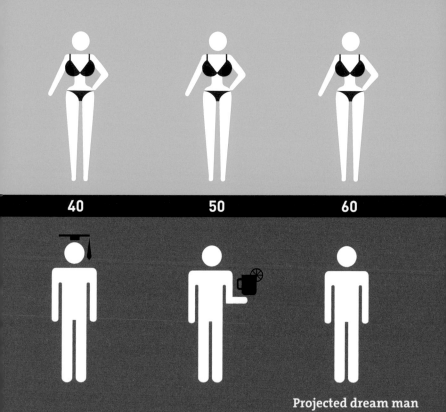

40   **50**   **60**

Projected dream man
Ihr Traummann · Homme de ses rêves · *El hombre de sus sueños*

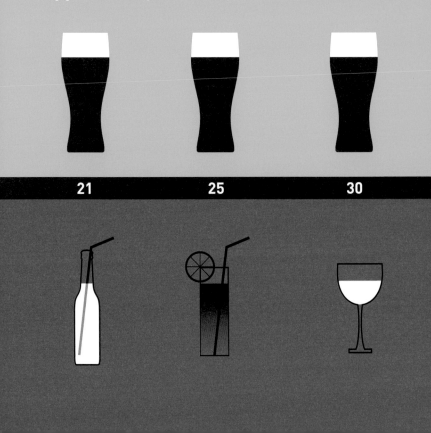

Favorite drink
Lieblingsgetränk · **Boisson préférée** · *Bebida preferida*

21 **25** **30**

35 40 50

Favorite drink
Lieblingsgetränk · **Boisson préférée** · *Bebida preferida*

Ideal age for marriage

Vorstellung vom idealen Heiratsalter · Âge idéal pour se marier · *Edad ideal para casarse*

25	30	40
18	25	30
18	25	30

50   60   18

40   50   60

40   50   60

Ideal age for marriage

Vorstellung vom idealen Heiratsalter · Âge idéal pour se marier · *Edad ideal para casarse*

Love
Liebe · Amour · Amor

Marriage

Heirat · **Mariage** · *Matrimonio*

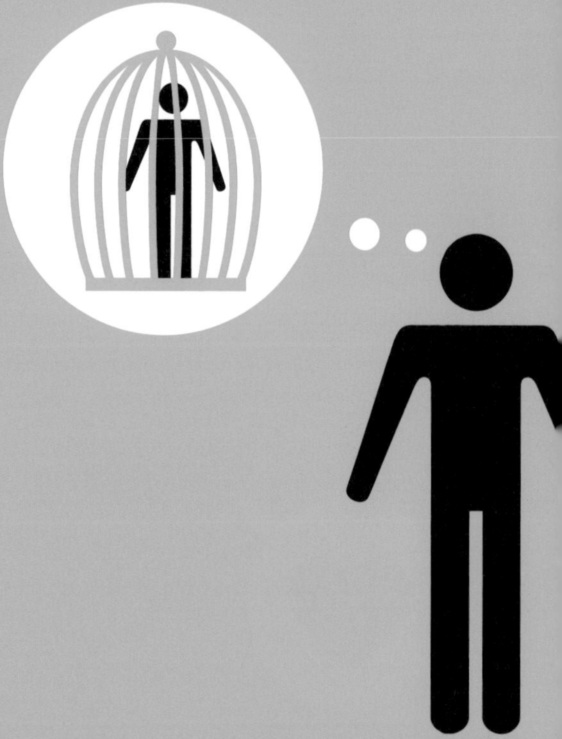

Marriage

Heirat · **Mariage** · *Matrimonio*

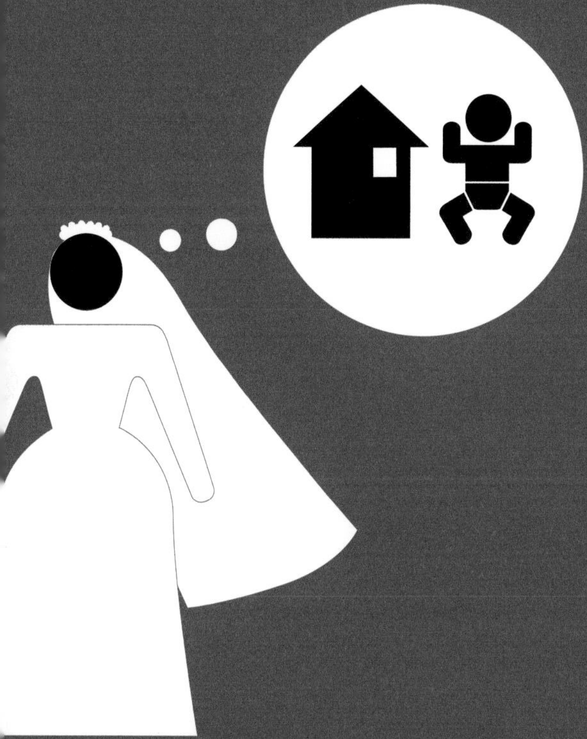

Speaking about children
Über Kinder sprechen · **Parler d'enfants** · *Hablando de tener hijos*

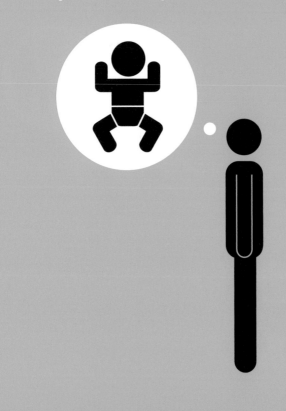

During pregnancy

Während der Schwangerschaft · Pendant la grossesse · *Durante el embarazo*

Baby
Das Baby · **Enfant** · *El bebé*

Baby

Das Baby · **Enfant** · *El bebé*

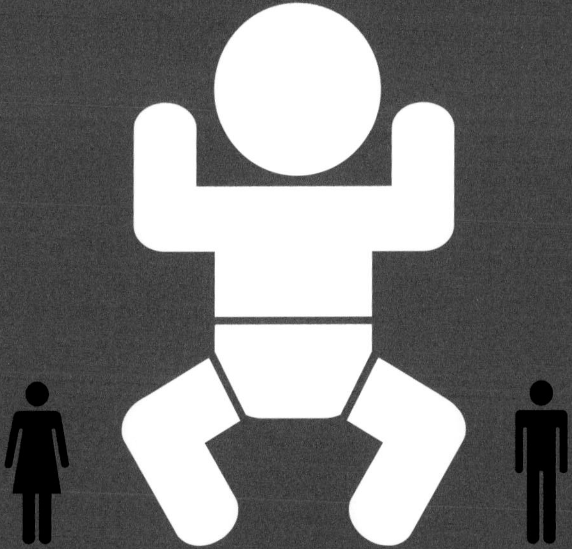

Baby arrives
Das Baby ist da! · Bébé est arrivé ! · *¡El bebé está en camino!*

before
vorher
avant
antes

after
nachher
après
después

Baby arrives
Das Baby ist da! · Bébé est arrivé ! · *¡El bebé está en camino!*

before
vorher
avant
antes

after
nachher
après
después

Social presence – man loves man

Gesellschaftliche Präsenz – Mann liebt Mann · Visibilité sociale – deux hommes qui s'aimer

Presencia social – amor entre hombres

Social presence – woman loves woman
Gesellschaftliche Präsenz – Frau liebt Frau · Visibilité sociale – deux femmes qui s'aiment
Presencia social – amor entre mujeres

He wants him
Er will ihn · **Il le veut** · *Él lo desea*

Men's magazine

Männerzeitschrift · **Magazines masculins** · *Revistas masculinas*

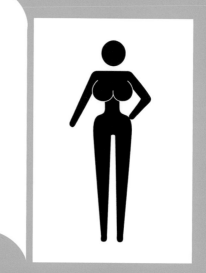

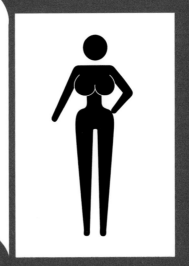

Competition
Wettbewerb · **Compétition** · *Competición*

Competition
Wettbewerb · **Compétition** · *Competición*

Successful man's prospects

Erfolgreicher Mann sucht Partnerin · Conquêtes de l'homme à succès

Expectativas de un triunfador

Successful woman's prospects

Erfolgreiche Frau sucht Partner · Conquêtes de la femme à succès

Expectativas de una triunfadora

Dream woman
Traumfrau · Idéal féminin · *Mujer ideal*

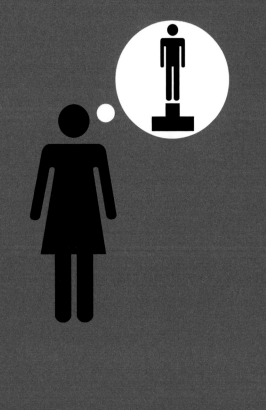

Dream man

Traummann · **Idéal masculin** · *Hombre ideal*

Dream woman of a successful man

Traumfrau des erfolgreichen Mannes · Idéal féminin de l'homme à succès
Mujer ideal de un hombre con éxito

Dream man of a successful woman
Traummann der erfolgreichen Frau · Idéal masculin de la femme à succès
Hombre ideal de una mujer con éxito

Salary expectations
Gehaltsvorstellung · **Prétentions salariales** · *Aspiraciones económicas*

Preferred boss
Bevorzugter Chef · **Chef idéal** · *Jefe ideal*

Preferred boss

Bevorzugter Chef · Chef idéal · *Jefe ideal*

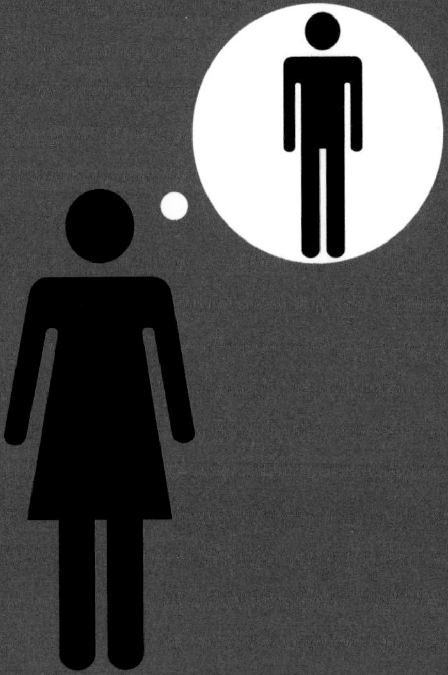

Family man
Familienvater · **Père de famille** · *Padre de familia*

Workaholic

Rabenmutter · Mordue du travail · *Adicta al trabajo*

Prince Charming
Charmeur · Séducteur · *Ligón*

Whore
Flittchen · Fille facile · *Prostituta*

Modern man
Moderner Mann · **Homme moderne** · *Hombre moderno*

Housewife
Heimchen am Herd · Mère au foyer · *Ama de casa*

Violent
Gewalttätig · Violence · Violencia

Feisty
Temperamentvoll · Tempérament · *Temperamento*

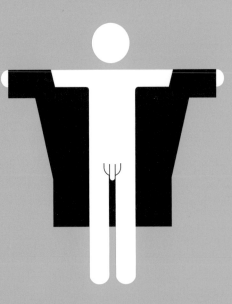

Creepy
Krank · **Malade** · *Enfermo*

Sexy
Sexy · Sexy · *Sexi*

Pervert
Pervers · **Perversion** · *Pervertido*

Bold
Gewagt · Culot · *Atrevida*

Macho
Macho · **Macho** · *Machista*

Strong woman
Starke Frau · Femme forte · *Mujer con carácter*

Weird man

Komischer Mann · **Homme bizarre** · *Hombre raro*

Normal woman
Normale Frau · Femme normale · *Mujer normal*

He thinks that she thinks...
Er denkt, dass sie denkt...
Il pense qu'elle pense...
Él piensa que ella piensa...

She thinks that he thinks...
Sie denkt, dass er denkt ...
Elle pense qu'il pense ...
Ella piensa que él piensa...

In 2008 I had the idea of making a book about the differences between the sexes. I wanted to take stock of my thoughts and observations on the subject of Man/Woman as a way of documenting another stage of my life. It took six years for the book to assume its final shape.

We are living in an age of constant social change, in which the subject of the sexes, in particular, is rapidly evolving in people's consciousness. Each new generation reassesses and questions the role models currently in place. All over the world, people are striving to break down existing structures and are taking a stand for greater tolerance and equality, including in areas such as sexual orientation, culture, and religion.

It is interesting to see how Man/Woman clichés have indeed changed in our daily lives and to what extent the attributes that were assigned to the sexes in the past, often centuries ago, are still relevant in today's society. And to consider which desirable role models are already rooted in our thinking but are still in the process of transformation.

I hope to present a worthy successor to *East meets West* and to continue exchanging thoughts and ideas with my readers on this topic and many others.

2008 kam mir die Idee, ein Buch über die Unterschiede der Geschlechter zu machen. Ich wollte eine Bestandsaufnahme meiner Wahrnehmung zum Thema Mann/Frau vorlegen, um einen weiteren Lebensabschnitt für mich zu dokumentieren. Es dauerte sechs Jahre, bis das Buch seine endgültige Form angenommen hat.

Wir leben in einer Zeit des ständigen gesellschaftlichen Wandels, insbesondere das Thema der Geschlechter entwickelt sich rasant im Bewusstsein der Menschen. Vorhandene Rollenbilder werden von jeder Generation neu bewertet und in Frage gestellt. Weltweit streben Menschen nach einem Aufbrechen der vorhandenen Strukturen und treten ein für mehr Toleranz und Gleichberechtigung, auch in Bereichen wie der sexuellen Orientierung, der Kultur oder der Religion.

Es ist interessant zu sehen, wie sich die Klischees zum Thema Mann/Frau tatsächlich in unserem Alltag verändert haben und inwieweit die oft seit Jahrhunderten existierenden Attribute der Geschlechter doch auch in unserer heutigen Gesellschaft noch Relevanz haben. Und welche wünschenswerten Rollenmuster zwar bereits in unserem Bewusstsein Niederschlag gefunden haben, sich aber noch im Prozess der Umwandlung befinden.

Ich hoffe, damit eine würdige Fortsetzung von *East meets West* zu präsentieren und mit meinen Lesern über das Thema hinaus weiterhin im Austausch zu bleiben.

En 2008, j'ai eu l'idée de créer un livre sur les différences entre les sexes. Je voulais faire le point sur ma façon d'appréhender les divergences homme/femme afin de conserver une trace de cette nouvelle étape de ma vie. Il m'a fallu six ans pour donner au livre sa forme actuelle.

Nous vivons dans une société en perpétuelle mutation, notamment en matière de genre, avec une prise de conscience qui évolue à une vitesse folle. Les représentations traditionnelles des rôles sont remises en question par chaque nouvelle génération. Dans le monde entier, les individus aspirent à rompre avec les structures existantes et militent pour plus de tolérance et d'égalité, y compris concernant l'orientation sexuelle, la culture et la religion.

Il est intéressant de noter combien les clichés sur les différences entre l'homme et la femme ont évolué dans notre quotidien, même si certains attributs souvent séculaires associés aux deux sexes restent bien ancrés dans la société actuelle. Il est aussi important de souligner les modèles de rôles souhaitables déjà entrés dans les esprits mais encore en gestation dans les faits.

J'espère offrir une suite digne de *East meets West* et poursuivre les riches échanges échanges avec mes lecteurs sur de multiples sujets.

Fue en 2008 cuando nació la idea de hacer un libro sobre las diferencias entre los sexos. Quería recoger mis percepciones sobre el tema de los hombres y las mujeres para así documentar una nueva etapa de mi vida. Pasaron seis años hasta que el libro adquirió su forma definitiva.

Vivimos en una época de constantes cambios sociales, y especialmente el tema de los sexos ha experimentado una tremenda evolución en la conciencia de las personas. Cada generación reevalúa y cuestiona los roles vigentes. En todo el mundo la gente aspira a romper las estructuras existentes y aboga por una mayor tolerancia e igualdad, también en ámbitos como la orientación sexual, la cultura o la religión.

Resulta interesante ver cómo han cambiado los clichés sobre las diferencias entre hombres y mujeres en nuestro día a día, y hasta qué punto atributos de los sexos a menudo existentes desde hace siglos mantienen su relevancia en nuestra sociedad actual. Asimismo, es curioso constatar que los roles ya están arraigados en nuestras mentes pese a estar aún en proceso de transformación.

Espero que este libro sea una digna secuela de East meets West *y me permita seguir intercambiando pensamientos e ideas con mis lectores acerca de este y muchos otros temas.*

Other books by Yang Liu:

"An ideal gift and food for thought."
—*Stern*, Hamburg

"For a generation that increasingly uses emoticons that say much more than words, these books could be the future."
—*Show Daily*, New Delhi

Yang Liu was born in 1976 in Beijing and moved to Germany at the age of 13. After studying at the University of Arts Berlin (UdK), she worked as a designer in Singapore, London, Berlin, and New York. In 2004 she founded her own design studio, which she continues to run today. In addition to holding workshops and lectures at international conferences, she has taught at numerous universities in Germany and abroad. In 2010 she was appointed a professor at the BTK University of Applied Sciences in Berlin. Her works have won numerous prizes in international competitions and can be found in museums and collections all over the world.

Yang Liu lives and works in Berlin.

Photo: Detlef Eden

**EACH AND EVERY TASCHEN BOOK
PLANTS A SEED!**

TASCHEN is a carbon neutral publisher.
Each year, we offset our annual carbon
emissions with carbon credits at the
Instituto Terra, a reforestation program
in Minas Gerais, Brazil, founded by Lélia
and Sebastião Salgado. To find out more
about this ecological partnership, please
check: www.taschen.com/zerocarbon.

**Inspiration: unlimited.
Carbon footprint: zero.**

To stay informed about TASCHEN and our
upcoming titles, please subscribe to
our free magazine at www.taschen.com/
magazine, follow us on Instagram and
Facebook, or e-mail your questions
to contact@taschen.com.

Man meets Woman
A book by **Yang Liu**

Idea/Design © Yang Liu

© Copyright of all
artwork and text by
Yang Liu Design
Torstraße 185 · 10115 Berlin
www.yangliudesign.com

English translation: Karen Williams
French translation: Arnaud Briand
Spanish translation: Belinda Saile/
Lola Huete Machado

© 2022 TASCHEN GmbH
Hohenzollernring 53 · 50672 Cologne
www.taschen.com

Original edition:
© 2014 TASCHEN GmbH

ISBN 978-3-8365-9213-0

Printed in Slovakia